HISTORICAL AMERICAN LANDMARKS

From the Old North Church to the Santa Fe Trail

by C.B.Colby

Coward, McCann & Geoghegan   New York

Contents

Courtesy of Sleepy Hollow Restorations, Tarrytown, New York: Page 17. National Park Service, Department of the Interior, Washington, D.C.: Title page and pages, 3, 22, 23, 24, 30, 31, 32, 33, 34, 35, 36, 37, 42, 44, 45, 46, 47, 48. K. F. Lutz, courtesy American Flag House and Betsy Ross Memorial Association, Philadelphia, Pennsylvania: Page 25. United States Army: Pages 26, 29 (bottom). United States Military Academy, West Point, New York: Page 27. Argonne National Laboratory, United States Atomic Energy Commission: Page 28 (top). University of Chicago, Chicago, Illinois: Page 28 (bottom). United States Atomic Energy Commission, Washington, D.C.: Page 29 (top). New Mexico State Tourist Bureau: Page 43. Jamestown Foundation, Williamsburg, Virginia: Pages 38, 39, 40, 41. All other photos, including full color cover, by the author.

SBN: GB 698-30190-0
Fifth Impression

08 up

Library of Congress Catalog Card Number: 68-23857

Go Find Our History!

There are so many historic landmarks spread about our great land that it was difficult to undertake the selection of those for this book. Most of the oldest are naturally on the East Coast where much of our earliest history began.

From there, as our history, heritage, and population moved westward, circumstances and events began to produce new landmarks along the way. Some are natural landmarks that lured, guided, or protected the pioneer travelers as they moved westward. Others are the sites or ruins of their homes, trails, forts, battlegrounds, and final resting places. Each in its way is a part of our history and heritage.

I based my selection on the effect of the landmark, or the event which it represents, on our history, its importance to the area in which it is located, or its growing importance over the years. There will be arguments about some of my selections and omissions, for local pride can be enthusiastic and vocal, and it should be.

If this book does nothing more than arouse your curiosity as to what your own local landmarks might be and send you off to find and see them, I'll be delighted, for you will better understand your country, your state, and perhaps even your own neighborhood.

How many of you regularly pass statues, memorial parks, and historic markers without a thought or a pause to find out what they are all about? Take a moment or two to learn about them, and you may be amazed and proud to find out what important event or events may have taken place so close at hand. No village, no matter how small, is without a history.

History suddenly comes alive when you visit historic landmarks such as you will see on the following pages. They range from Revolutionary War battlefields and buildings, lovely old churches and humble huts, to more modern canals and memorials. They include some carved by nature and some carved lovingly by the talented hands of man. When you walk the same ground or turn the same doorknob that our nation's great have walked or touched, those events and those great men of our history will become more real to you.

There are hundreds of national landmarks and thousands of locally important ones, so there are plenty to be found and visited in every corner of our land and every state of the Union. Go and find them, perhaps with the help of your parents, your teacher, librarian, or Scout leader. If some of your local ones are unmarked, perhaps you can make a class or troop project out of seeing that they are properly identified so that others may share in the pride of knowing about them.

In my travels to take and collect the photographs and research material for this book I met and had the friendly cooperation of many persons. My warmest thanks and appreciation for their help, and a particular word of thanks to an old friend, Francis X. Kelly, of the National Park Service, Department of the Interior, Washington, D.C., and to Reverend G. Earl Daniels, Associate Vicar of the Old North Church of Boston, Massachusetts, who graciously permitted me to take interior photos of this beautiful old house of worship.

Traveling about the country in connection with the book renewed my belief in the growing interest and pride of Americans in our great heritage and its landmarks, for everywhere we went there were crowds of both young and old, reading inscriptions, looking, and taking photos. Go out and join them for many thrilling experiences and for an even greater pride in being a part of America's history.

C. B. COLBY

Plymouth Rock

Plymouth, Mass.

On December 21, 1620, the Pilgrims landed on the shores of Plymouth Bay in Massachusetts, about thirty-seven miles southeast of what is now Boston. They stepped ashore onto a small boulder on the rocky beach. This simple piece of stone has since become famous as Plymouth Rock and is one of America's first historic landmarks, a fitting introduction to this book. The stone, now resting on its original site on the shore, is protected from vandals and the weather by a portico of granite (opposite page, top). Visitors can see the rock by looking over the railing above it or by climbing down to the beach and peering through the bars at close range. Behind the columned portico rises Cole's Hill, where the first winter was spent. Many of those who died were buried on the level hilltop, upon which corn was planted "lest the Indians know how many were the graves." Above, the famous Plymouth Rock in its present home. During 1774, the year before the outbreak of the Revolutionary War, the rock became a symbol of freedom to the colonists and was dragged from its bed on the shore to Liberty Pole Square some distance away and was accidentally split in two. It has since been returned to its original spot and repaired. The photos opposite show reconstructed Pilgrim homes (center) and a replica of the *Mayflower* (bottom), both close by Plymouth Rock. The *Mayflower* seen here is really the *Mayflower II,* a replica of the original, which was given to the United States by England in 1957. The houses can be seen at the splendid reconstruction of "Plimoth Plantation," a short distance away from the rock and well worth a visit.

The Old North Church

Boston, Mass.

Everyone has heard of the famous ride of Paul Revere on the night of April 18, 1775, and how two lanterns were hung in the tower of this famous old Boston landmark, according to the order "One if by land and two if by sea." Above you can see the Old North Church in the background and the stirring statue of Paul Revere in the foreground, in a small park behind the church. On the opposite page are two views of the beautiful interior of the church. The upper photo shows the black and gold organ and the clock which has been running ever since it was built in 1726. Some of the organ pipes are originals dating from 1759 and are still functioning. In the lower photo, taken from just to the left of the organ, you can see the original brass chandelier (one of two), hanging from the ceiling since 1724. The church was begun in 1723. The first sermon preached there was from the text from Isaiah "For mine house shall be called a house of prayer for all people." The box pews helped keep the worshipers warm in winter. Each family brought hot bricks or hot coals in little tin footwarmers, as there was no heat in the church. The dark box pew (left) shows how all pews were originally lined to help keep them warm. Note the lovely raised pulpit and the unique sounding board suspended over it for better acoustics. The Old North Church is still a house of worship with regular services. It is open daily from 10 A.M. to 4 P.M.

Lexington Green

Lexington, Mass.

When the British marched from Boston to Concord to capture supplies stored there for the militia of the colonies, Paul Revere spread the alarm ahead of them. By the time they reached the village green in Lexington (shown above as it appears today) Captain John Parker had assembled about seventy minutemen there to face them. When some of his men saw the size of the approaching British force, they suggested that he withdraw, but he silenced them by saying, "Stand your ground! Don't fire unless fired upon! But if they mean to have war let it begin here!" When the British force of between six hundred and eight hundred regulars arrived, some of the minutemen began to drift away. Captain Parker, seeing the hopelessness of the situation, gave the order to disband. Almost at that moment someone fired a shot, someone unknown to this day. The British fired a return volley, cutting down Captain Parker's cousin Jonas and seventeen other minutemen. The rest broke up in confusion and the cheering British marched off to Concord, where they met their first casualties at the Concord Bridge. On the opposite page is the magnificent statue of the minuteman, by H. H. Kitson, at the point of the triangular green. Farther back, marking the line of minutemen on the green, a granite boulder rests. On this boulder is carved a musket and powderhorn and the fighting words of Captain Parker. The tall flagpole bears the legend "Birthplace of American Liberty."

Concord Bridge

"By the rude bridge that arched the flood, their flag to April's breeze unfurled, here once the embattled farmers stood, and fired the shot heard round the world." This inscription, known to most schoolchildren, is carved on the famous statue of the minuteman at Concord Bridge, near Concord, Massachusetts. The local minutemen, warned by Paul Revere that the British were coming, had gathered across this bridge on the morning of April 19, 1775. The Redcoats, after setting the Concord courthouse afire, met them there. The British, believing that the minutemen would not dare fight, planned on holding the bridge. At the first British volley the minutemen fired back, killing and wounding several British soldiers, and the fight was over. Above are two views of the "rude bridge that arched the flood" and opposite, the statue of the farmer-soldier, placed where the colonial forces stood, one hand on his plow and the other holding his musket. The name "minuteman" came from the fact that he was supposed to be ready to fight at a minute's notice. The statue was by Daniel Chester French (page 32).

From the British Side

This is a view of the famed Concord Bridge, taken from where the British stood and challenged the colonial minutemen. Here the first enemy soldiers fell to flintlock muskets in the hands of the aroused farmers of Concord, Acton, Lincoln, and Bedford, led by Major John Buttrick. To the left of this simple monument are the graves of the British soldiers who fell, marked by a bronze plaque. Situated as it is, it is difficult to photograph clearly (opposite page, top) but the inscription reads: "Grave of British Soldiers: They came three thousand miles and died to keep the past upon its throne; unheard beyond the ocean tide, their English mother made her moan. April 19, 1775." Just beyond the stone wall of which this plaque is a part stands the Old Manse built in 1769 (lower photo, opposite). This well-preserved old homestead was lived in by several early literary figures, of which the most famous were Nathaniel Hawthorne, Ralph Waldo Emerson, and Reverend George Ripley. The Reverend Ripley was one of the first exponents of socialism in America. This whole area of Massachusetts is steeped in early American history and dotted with famous landmarks to visit.

GRAVE OF BRITISH SOLDIERS
THEY CAME THREE THOUSAND MILES AND DIED
TO KEEP THE PAST UPON ITS THRONE
UNHEARD BEYOND THE OCEAN TIDE
THEIR ENGLISH MOTHER MADE HER MOAN

Paul Revere's House

Boston, Mass.

Within easy walking distance of the famed Old North Church stands the interesting house that Paul Revere lived in. This house was built around 1677 and is the oldest house in Boston. It was almost a century old in 1770 when Paul Revere moved in. He lived here for thirty years until 1800. It was from here that he left for the Boston Tea Party in 1773 and set out on his historic ride on the night of April 18, 1775. This house is one of the highlights of the Freedom Trail, a walking tour of famous historic shrines in Boston. It is a small house with low ceilings, furnished with authentic pieces from the time of Revere. In one of the bedrooms there is a lovely four-poster bed, and standing by it is one of the original posts from Paul Revere's bed. Over the living room mantelpiece is an interesting old sword found in the house when it was restored. Several original cooking utensils and kitchen devices are to be seen in the kitchen. In another room there is a unique coattail chair, designed with a triangular seat and back so a man's coattails could stick out behind on either side of the back. The house is open to the public, and visitors find it fascinating.

Old Dutch Church

North Tarrytown, N.Y.

The whole area around Tarrytown, New York, up the Hudson River from New York City, is steeped in early history. This region was also the birthplace of the famous legends of Sleepy Hollow and the Headless Horseman, written by Washington Irving. This early Dutch church, also shown on the cover in full color, was built about 1699, as the tablet on the front of it states, but there is some question as to the exact year. When first built, it had seven windows; now there are six. The original windows were seven feet above the ground so that the Indians could not look in. The walls were thirty inches thick so the church could be used as a fort in case of attack. The interior is simple and severe. Behind the church, shown in the photo above, is a graveyard containing the graves and markers of many parish members of Revolutionary and earlier times. One unmarked burial close to the wall of the church is that of Hulda, the "witch," a Bohemian woman who lived alone in the Sleepy Hollow woods in the 1770's. Shunned by all, she finally won their respect and a Christian burial close by the old church by fighting along with the colonists against the British who were marching against the colonial general Israel Putnam in Peekskill. Her little store of gold was left to the widows of the men who fell for their country. This beautiful and historic Dutch church was part of the manor of Fredryk Flypse, a large shipowner, trader, and landowner of that period. A restoration of his manor house, now known as Philipsburg Manor, Upper Mills, is within walking distance of this historic landmark.

More About Sleepy Hollow

The cemetery behind the Old Dutch Church continues up the slope behind it, along the old Albany Post Road (now Route 9), to the Revolutionary War redoubt at the top of the little hill, where the trenches are still visible (top) among the headstones. The monument bears the names of the men who fought there. Between the church and this redoubt is located the Irving family plot. Here Washington Irving (1783–1859), famed author of the Sleepy Hollow tales, is buried with many others of his famous family. Some of the stones are so weather-worn that they are impossible to read, but many bear dates of more than a century ago. On the opposite page is Sunnyside, Washington Irving's home, a few miles to the south of where he is buried.

Washington Irving's Sunnyside

Tarrytown, New York

High on a bank above the Hudson stands this mansion with its stepped-gable roof, the home of Washington Irving. The famous author purchased this property in 1835, when it was a simple country home, nothing like it appears now. In about 1835 and 1837 he remodeled and enlarged the original building into what became a show-place of the vicinity. It still is. Irving often referred to this picturesque mansion as his snuggery, and he invited many famous literary friends there for stimulating get-togethers. Among them were such famous names as Oliver Wendell Holmes, Nathaniel Hawthorne, Henry Wadsworth Longfellow, Ralph Waldo Emerson, James Fenimore Cooper, William Cullen Bryant, and John P. Kennedy. This famous land-mark is located on the borderline of Tarrytown and Irvington, New York, about twenty-five miles north of New York City. The smaller photo shows Irving's study where he wrote many of his famous Sleepy Hollow tales. Sunnyside is furnished with a number of original antiques, many of them from the Irving family and among them are many personal belongings of the author. The mansion is open to the public.

Where Washington Crossed the Delaware

One of the greatest boosts to the American cause during the Revolutionary War was the capture of Trenton, New Jersey, the day after Christmas in 1776. Earlier that month Washington and his men had been pushed westward across the Delaware River by the troops of General Howe on their way to capture Philadelphia. All that lay between the British and their target was the river. Fortunately, Washington and his men had taken all the boats for miles upstream and down across the river with them so General Howe was forced to stop at Trenton. In one last desperate effort General Washington and a force of ragged troops, some barefoot, crossed the ice-choked Delaware in Durham ore boats and marched nine miles in sleet and snow to Trenton, arriving there in the early morning hours of the day after Christmas. They captured the town and routed the British without the loss of a single American life. Today you can look across that same spot where these brave men crossed (above) and visit the fine museum and theater above and behind it (opposite page, top). The center photo shows the point of embarkation marked with stone monuments and the lower photo, one of the Durham boats manned by seafaring men from Marblehead, Massachusetts, who ferried the troops and their equipment through the ice floes. These sturdy ore boats were forty to sixty feet long and could carry up to fifteen tons. The victory at Trenton was America's first victory as a new nation and one that was a turning point on our way to eventual independence and freedom.

Valley Forge

Pennsylvania

The cruelest winter for American troops was that of 1777–1778, spent at Valley Forge in Pennsylvania. A heart-stricken General Washington wrote of his troops, "To see men without clothes to cover their nakedness, without blankets to lie on, without shoes, for want of which their marches might be traced by the blood from their feet, and almost as often without provisions as with them . . . is proof of patience and obedience which in my opinion can scarce be paralleled." This great area, where so many thousands of American patriots endured unbelievable hardships for their ideal of freedom and independence, must be visited to be understood. The photo above shows a street of reconstructed log huts, similar to those in which Washington's men spent that winter. The opposite page (top) shows General Washington's headquarters, which is filled with many original objects from the period and personal items of the General and his staff. The lower photo shows some of the many authentic Revolutionary War cannon that may be seen in batteries about the area. There are many historic buildings, observation points, redoubts, and huts within the Valley Forge memorial. Signs and maps bring the area to life for the visitor as he walks among the original and reconstructed buildings and shelters of this great and tragic American landmark.

Independence Hall

Philadelphia, Penn.

Independence Hall, originally the statehouse for the province of Pennsylvania, is considered one of the most beautiful public buildings of the colonial period. It is located in an area of Philadelphia which is being developed as an extensive section of colonial reconstruction. Many old buildings are being restored or reconstructed to make that portion of the city a living museum of what the area looked like in colonial times. Independence Hall was begun in the spring of 1732 and finally finished in the 1750's. Inside you can see many beautiful examples of colonial furniture and paneling. It also houses the famed Liberty Bell, located almost directly inside the center door shown in the photo above. The photo opposite (top) shows the reconstructed Assembly Room in Independence Hall, where the Declaration of Independence was signed on July 4, 1776. The lower photo shows the Liberty Bell with its famous inscription from Leviticus: "Proclaim liberty throughout all the land unto all the inhabitants thereof." The bell is one of America's most treasured symbols. The statue in the photo above is of Commodore John Barry (1745–1803), famous Revolutionary soldier and captain of naval ships. He is known as the "Father of our Navy."

Carpenters' Hall
Philadelphia, Penn.

Carpenters' Hall was built in 1770 for use as a guild hall by the Carpenters' Company of Philadelphia. On September 5, 1774, the First Continental Congress met here to determine what measures the colonies should take to resist Britain's oppressive colonial policies. The delegates had been offered the use of the Pennsylvania statehouse (Independence Hall) but decided to meet in the recently completed Carpenters' Hall instead, thus giving it a place in history. The Carpenters' Company is still an active organization and uses its venerable and historic hall for regular meetings and functions. This fine example of colonial architecture is located on Chestnut Street, just a few minutes' walk from Independence Hall, and is part of the historic section of Philadelphia. It contains many rare antiques, paintings, and colonial artifacts.

Betsy Ross House

Philadelphia, Penn.

The story of how Betsy Ross made the first Stars and Stripes is one of the most popular of American legends. According to one version told by her descendants General Washington, Robert Morris, and General George Ross came to her small upholstery shop to see if she could make a flag for the American forces. She replied that she had never made one but would try. They gave her a rough design which included six-pointed stars instead of five-pointed stars. She suggested that five-pointed stars would look better. They agreed but said the six-pointed ones would be easier to make, whereupon she demonstrated how perfect five-pointed stars could be made with a folded piece of material and a single cut of the scissors. Washington was delighted, changed the sketch, and left with the other two gentlemen. The flag was soon finished and approved. It had thirteen stars in a circle on a field of blue and is often called the Betsy Ross Flag. This flag is still legal and may be flown in place of the present flag. No real documentary proof has ever been presented to prove this story but it has been generally accepted. However we know that a Mrs. John Ross (1752–1836) did live in Philadelphia and that she was an upholsterer and flagmaker by trade. A flag always flies over her grave in Mount Moriah Cemetery. A small colonial house at 239 Arch Street, within walking distance of Independence Hall, is known as the Betsy Ross House and is furnished with furniture of that period. A Betsy Ross Flag, flying from an upper window, welcomes the public to this popular landmark.

West Point

New York

Of the historic American landmarks associated with the military, perhaps the most familiar and impressive is West Point, where the United States Military Academy is located. Many people do not realize that this site was originally a fort to protect the Hudson River from invasion by the British during the Revolutionary War. It was this fort that General Benedict Arnold planned to betray to the British. It is the oldest continually manned military post in the country and has never been captured. The Academy itself was founded in 1803 with ten cadets and five officers, for it was obvious from the Revolutionary War that trained officers were desperately needed for our Regular Army. Today graduates of the Point, as it is affectionately called, serve in every corner of the globe. Its military museum is one of the best in the world and along with the many military monuments, cannon, and buildings makes the Point a fascinating place to visit. Above is a photo of how the Point looks today high on a plateau above the Hudson. You can see the river in the upper left corner of the photo. On the opposite page is a drawing of how it looked in 1825 (top) and (lower) one of the batteries of cannon facing upriver in 1866.

Stagg Field

Not all historic American landmarks date from colonial days. Some are as new as the Atomic Age. History need not be yesterday's events, for if it is important enough, what happens today can establish an American landmark for the future. For example, under the crumbling stands of Stagg Field at the University of Chicago the first sustained nuclear chain reaction was accomplished on December 2, 1942, and ushered in the Atomic Age. Although the stands under which this historic event took place are no longer there, the site is marked with a unique and almost foreboding sculpture by Henry Moore. The photo above shows the west stands of Stagg Field under which the first continuous nuclear chain reaction took place. The smaller photo shows a model of the sculpture which marks this historic site.

First Atomic Explosion Site   Alamogordo, New Mexico

On the morning of July 16, 1945, at 5:30 A.M., the sky over Alamogordo, New Mexico, was lighted by the brightest light ever made by man, and the awful power of the atom turned loose became a reality. The atomic device was detonated on top of a steel tower surrounded by scientific equipment. The equipment was remotely monitored by instruments watched by scientists nearly six miles away in concrete bunkers. The explosion vaporized the steel tower and fused the surrounding desert sand into glass for a radius of eight hundred yards from the tower base, or "point zero." Here was first seen the characteristic mushroom cloud of nuclear explosions. Here too men first fully realized the terrific impact this force would have on the future of mankind. At the top of the page is a historic photo of this first atomic explosion and below this, the site of this awesome event as it appears today in the desert. The site, officially designated a historic spot in American history, is located in one section of the White Sands Missile Range, Socorro County, New Mexico.

Ford's Theater

Washington, D.C.

Several of our national landmarks are unfortunately associated with tragedies. Perhaps the one most remembered for the tragic circumstances which made it a historic site is the old Ford's Theater on Tenth Street in our nation's capital. On the night of April 14, 1865, President Abraham Lincoln went to the theater with Mrs. Lincoln, accompanied by Major H. R. Rathbone, his military aide, and Miss Clara Harris, Rathbone's fiancée, the daughter of Senator Ira Harris of New York. They were to see a comedy entitled *Our American Cousin* and to hear a special song "Honor to Our Soldiers" in honor of the soldiers of the Civil War, which had just been concluded. Some time after ten o'clock John Wilkes Booth, who had long planned the assassination, entered the presidential box and shot the President. He escaped across the stage. Ford's Theater, now completely restored, is open to the public. Above, you can see Ford's Theater as it looks today and on opposite page, the house just across the street where Lincoln died the following morning. It was owned by a tailor named Peterson. It was there that Secretary Stanton exclaimed, "Now he belongs to the ages."

Lincoln Memorial

Washington, D.C.

Those of you who have stood before this magnificent and moving statue of the martyred Lincoln may have wondered what he might see from his position. In this unusual photo by Abbie Rowe you look down upon the memorial entrance and some of those visitors who come to pay tribute. On the opposite page is a splendid view of this great piece of sculpture. It is by Daniel Chester French, the same talented sculptor who just fifty years before at the age of twenty-two had completed the statue of the minuteman standing by Concord Bridge (page 11). When the Lincoln Memorial and its statue was dedicated in 1922, French was seventy-two years old. He was born in Exeter, New Hampshire, in 1850 and died in 1931. The building in which the statue is sheltered was designed by Henry Bacon. It includes thirty-six fluted columns, representing the thirty-six states in the Union at the time of Lincoln's death. Located in Potomac Park, the Lincoln Memorial is one of our nation's most beautiful historic landmarks.

The Smithsonian Institution   *Washington, D.C.*

In order to properly see one of Washington's and the nation's most interesting and extensive landmarks you must climb to the top of the famed Washington Monument (opposite page) and look toward the national Capitol, another familiar landmark. Below you on the right side of the long mall is a dark castlelike building, and opposite it are three huge buildings, two with small domed portions of their roofs and one (lower left) with a level roof. They are all part of the same landmark complex, the fantastic Smithsonian Institution. In all there are ten blocks, occupied by seven buildings, plus the National Zoological Park a few miles away. The Smithsonian Institution was made possible by the unusual gift of roughly half a million dollars through the will of James Smithson, an Englishman who had never visited the United States. This gentleman left the money to a nephew with the stipulation that if this nephew died without any children, the money was to go to the United States "to found at Washington, under the name of the Smithsonian Institution, an establishment for the increase and diffusion of knowledge among men." The nephew did die childless in 1835, and the money came to America to finance the beginning of this tremendous complex of buildings. They now include the original building, often referred to as the castle, a red-brick structure with many towers and minarets, the Museum of History and Technology (lower left-hand corner), the Natural History Building (beyond this with dark round dome), and the National Gallery of Art

(second building with white dome). The buildings immediately behind the castle are also part of the Smithsonian Institution. Today there are over 57,000,000 items in its various collections. While only a fraction of them can be displayed at one time, the various exhibits are continually being changed and brought up to date by a highly skilled and imaginative staff of experts. The exhibits range from priceless gems and antiques through the gowns of Presidents' wives to aircraft and spacecraft. Besides the Washington complex of buildings and zoo, the Smithsonian Institution also maintains the Canal Zone Biological Area, a four-thousand-acre reserve on Barro Colorado Island in Gatun Lake in the Panama Canal Zone, as well as an astrophysical observatory and many other departments and international services. All of these do truly contribute to "the increase and diffusion of knowledge among men." If ever in our capital, do not fail to visit some of the various portions of this national landmark, for it is an education in itself and an exhibition that could take many exciting weeks to see.

Chesapeake and Ohio Canal

Before railroads became common, the best means of transportation westward, other than by covered wagon, was by one of the many canals Americans had dug across the fields and forests. Today most of them are abandoned with the exception of a very few which have been widened and deepened and equipped with modern locks. One of the few which have been left as they were, as historic landmarks, is the Chesapeake and Ohio Canal, planned by George Washington in the 1780's and completed in 1850. This picturesque canal ran 185 miles from the Georgetown section of Washington, D.C., to Cumberland, Maryland. It was an important commercial waterway during the latter part of the nineteenth century, but its traffic ceased about the turn of the century. At present, eight and a half miles, from Georgetown to Seneca, Maryland, have been restored by the National Park Service. Mule-drawn canal boats take sightseers up and down the picturesque waterway every Saturday and Sunday. Above is a view of the old Pennyfield locks and lockhouse and on opposite page (top), one of the passenger barges and its one-mule power engine. The center photo shows the Monocacy Aqueduct where the C & O Canal passes over a natural stream. The lower photo shows a scene along the abandoned but still interesting part of the canal, and an old lock.

Jamestown

America's first permanent English settlement began in May, 1607, when three tiny ships arrived from England and anchored off the Virginia coast. The colonists christened the river James and founded Jamestown. There were 120 men and boys (some reports say 104 men and boys) in the party. They at once built a triangular fort for protection against the Indians and Spaniards. Disease, starvation, and warfare with the Indians almost wiped out this first colony. Other colonists arrived from time to time, which only added to the general misery of the settlement. Eventually, under the unexpected leadership of Captain John Smith of the original party, the colony did flourish and become a well-organized and secured settlement. This site has been splendidly reconstructed in great detail, along with accurate replicas of the three ships which carried the colonists across the ocean. Above is an aerial view of the stockade fort and grass-thatched cabins of the first settlement, and on the opposite page is a close-up of a cannon port in the stockade wall of Fort James. The guard, uniformed in the style of the men of that period, carries a wooden-shafted halberd. Such foot soldiers were known as halberdiers. Outside the walls of Fort James are reconstructed Indian lodges and a glassblowers' building, where America's first industry, glassblowing, was begun in 1608. Daily demonstrations of this art are still given.

38

More About Jamestown

A fascinating part of the Jamestown restoration is the fleet of three ships in which the first colonists arrived in 1607. These are perfect replicas with the exception of the recent addition of fiber glass bottoms for longer life. They are shown above, looking more like toys than the actual ships in which over a hundred hardy souls crossed the ocean. Compared with the oceangoing ships of today, they are frighteningly small. Left to right they are the *Susan Constant,* 100 tons and about 76 feet long, the *Godspeed,* 40 tons and about 50 feet long, and the tiny *Discovery,* 20 tons and only 38 feet long. Visitors may board the flagship *Susan Constant* and inspect the cramped quarters in which the colonists endured their voyage of many months. On the opposite page is shown the original tower of the historic Jamestown brick church of 1639. A memorial church adjoining the tower was built in 1907 over the foundations of an even earlier church, in which the first representative legislative assembly in America was convened on July 30, 1619. A visit to this historic landmark area will give you a new interest in how our great nation began.

Fort Bowie

Arizona

The scattered ruins dotting the barren landscape shown in the two photos above are all that is left of an exciting historic landmark once of vital importance to western travelers, Fort Bowie. The most dangerous point on the early stage route to California was Apache Pass between the Dos Cabezas and the Chiricahua mountains. At the eastern end of this dangerous pass was built this adobe fort, barracks, store, and homes. All that remains of this once thriving military outpost are these ruins where once attacks by Cochise, Victorio, and Geronimo brought terror to the travelers. Fort Bowie is located in Cochise County, Arizona, near the present towns of Wilcox and Bowie, and in the area of the Chiricahua National Monument. It is quite difficult to reach, as the area is most desolate, but as a historical landmark it is worthy of consideration among those perhaps better known and handier to the landmark hunter.

Shiprock

New Mexico

Several years ago, while traveling through the western part of New Mexico, we could see ahead of us a towering mass of jagged rock against the skyline. For hours this towering shape grew larger as we continued toward the northwest corner of the state. I wondered how many pioneers had also seen that towering landmark and had headed toward it as a point of destination. When we reached the town of Shiprock, New Mexico, in the extreme northwestern corner of the state in a Navajo Indian reservation, we could see it at close range. We learned that this towering outcrop of rock had in truth been a landmark for countless westward-bound pioneers. It was also venerated by the Indians as the Great Winged Bird which had brought their ancestors to the land. Towering as it does out of the vast plains of that area, it is small wonder that it served as an important landmark for the pioneers as well as for the Indians. Many pioneers drew their wagons into a protective circle under the shadow of this great rock formation, which to them resembled a huge distant ship under full sail, hence its name.

Chimney Rock and Scotts Bluff   Nebraska

The westward-bound pioneers had to use physical landmarks almost more than maps, for in many cases the maps that they had were not very reliable. They followed the ruts of previous pioneer wagons, picking up visible landmarks, such as Shiprock and the towering Chimney Rock shown above. This natural landmark rises five hundred feet above the North Platte river valley. It was a familiar and popular landmark and campsite for the great migration west, along the Oregon and Mormon Trails. Chimney Rock was one of the first landmarks on the Oregon Trail, twenty-five miles east of Scotts Bluff and just across the North Platte River from what is now Bayard, Nebraska. On the opposite page is a photo of the wagon ruts cut down through the rock by countless steel-shod wagons rolling westward. This area is now the Scotts Bluff National Monument, and anyone interested in the pioneers will find here many traces of the great migration to California and Oregon. The three Boy Scouts are walking in the trough cut by the wagons, near Mitchell Pass, within the Scotts Bluff National Monument.

The Santa Fe Trail Ruts   **Colorado**

The Sante Fe Trail, which ran from Independence, Missouri, across the broad plains to Santa Fe, New Mexico, and then on down into Mexico, was the scene of much of our early western history. It was an important commercial route for over half a century, from 1821 to 1880. It is quite possible that the Spaniards used this route as early as 1541. Not only did the poorly equipped pioneers use this route, but heavily laden wagons of trading goods, including hardware and dry goods, rumbled over it. After leaving its terminus in Missouri (Franklin, Independence, and then later, Westport), the trail headed west in an almost straight line for eight hundred miles before branching into two routes, west and south, and then meeting again northeast of Santa Fe. In many places the wagon ruts of this historic old trail can still be seen, and some of the old stage stations are still in quite good condition. Above is the Sapello stage station near La Junta, Colorado, on the Arkansas River. On the opposite page (top) is a view of the old stage and wagon ruts south of Fort Union, just outside of Watrous, New Mexico. The lower photo shows more of these ruts (dark area in the middle distance). Beyond them the ruins of the old fort itself show as a row of dark dots below the mountain. Some portions of this historic old trail can still be traveled.

The Statue of Liberty   *New York*

One American landmark that has particular appeal to many millions is the Statue of Liberty, holding aloft her torch above New York Harbor. Given to the United States by France in 1884, she has been the symbol of freedom for countless millions of emigrants coming to America to find a new life and true freedom. The purpose of this colossal gift was to commemorate the birth of the United States and the continuing friendship between the people of the French and American democracies. The sculptor was Frédéric Auguste Bartholdi. It was he who recommended that the statue be placed on a tiny twelve-acre island in the harbor, then known as Bedloe's Island. In 1960 it was officially renamed Liberty Island. The statue was dedicated October 28, 1886. This historic figure is 151 feet high, plus another 154 feet for the pedestal. Total height is 305 feet plus a few inches. The observation platform in the statue's head is 260 feet above sea level and holds forty persons. When visitors were permitted to climb into her raised torch through the arm, another twelve persons could look out from the torch. This has now been discontinued as too dangerous. The figure is covered with over 300 sheets of copper 3/32 inch thick, and the entire statue weighs 450,000 pounds. This famed statue is an official national monument and one of our most famous historic landmarks, truly a fitting last page to this book of so many we can be proud of.